D1154296

Books by Carl E. Hiller

FROM TEPEES TO TOWERS: A Photographic History
    of American Architecture

BABYLON TO BRASILIA: The Challenge of City Planning

Babylon to Brasilia
The Challenge of City Planning

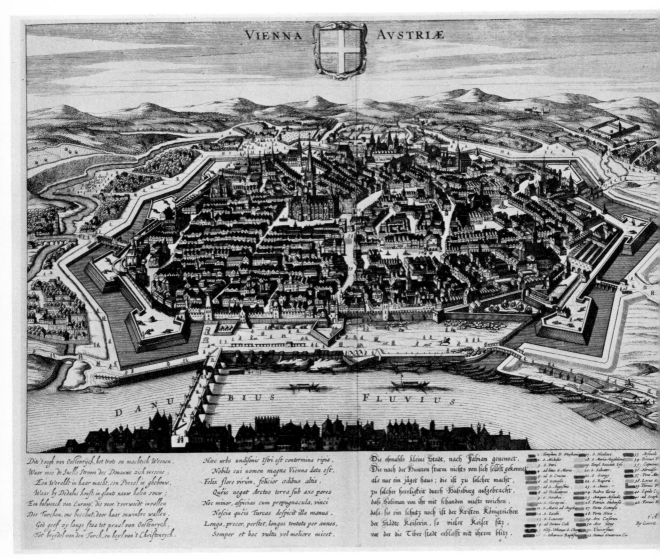

The city of Vienna as it appeared in the seventeenth century, surrounded by walls and a moat. A street called the Ringstrasse now
circles the inner city in place of the wall shown here.

Babylon to Brasilia

The Challenge of City Planning

by Carl E. Hiller

LITTLE, BROWN AND COMPANY
Boston   Toronto

Published simultaneously in Canada
by Little, Brown & Company (Canada) Limited

PRINTED IN THE UNITED STATES OF AMERICA

To the memory of
James Edward Tobin

Acknowledgments

FOR THEIR ADVICE, help, and encouragement in the preparation of this book the author wishes to thank Alden Aust, Edmund N. Bacon, C. Gates Beckwith, Arthur Boodaghian, Henry Chafetz, William Duprey, Herbert Emmerich, Edwin Friedman, Lawrence C. Goldsmith, William Hennelly, Hinman Kealy, Rose Lehrer, Anand Mohan, Gerd Muehsam, Martha Munzer, Sylvia Noroff, Nettie Osofsky, Neal Richmond, John Riess, Clarence S. Stein, Florence Weintraub, Marjean McConnell Willett, and Zeke Ziner.

Contents

	Acknowledgments	*viii*
	Introduction	3
	What's Wrong with Our Cities?	5
I	A Short History of Cities	17
	Why Do People Live in Cities?	17
	Where and How Did Cities Grow?	21
	The Form of Cities	25
	What Has Happened to Cities?	27
	What Can Be Done to Cure the City's Ills?	29
2	Plans and Planners	37
	L'Enfant and the City of Washington	37
	Haussmann and the Rebuilding of Paris	40
	Ebenezer Howard and His Garden Cities	43
	Broadacre City: An Idea of Frank Lloyd Wright	46
	Le Corbusier: Two Dreams and a Reality	48
	Chandigarh: Le Corbusier's Chance	50
	Islamabad: A New Capital for a New State	52
	Brasilia: The Story of a Vision	54
3	The New Town Movement around the World	58
	New Towns in the United States	59
	Reston and Columbia: Cities in Parks	62
	Cumbernauld: One of Britain's New Towns	64
	Tapiola: Garden City of Finland	66
	Nuns' Island: Montreal's New City	68
4	Putting New Life into Old Cities	71
	Rotterdam	72

Urban Renewal: U.S.A.   74

   Philadelphia   75

   Pittsburgh's Golden Triangle   82

   Omaha   84

   New York's Battery Park City   87

5   Ideas for the Future   90

   Seward's Success: Climate Control in Alaska   90

   The Domed City: Fuller's Dream   92

   Stratasystem: A Plan for Tomorrow   94

Glossary   97

Sources of Illustrations   100

Bibliography   101

List of Institutions Offering Programs in City Planning   103

Index   107

Babylon to Brasilia

The Challenge of City Planning

Part of the city of Bath in western England. Most of the houses in this picture were built in the Georgian style of the eighteenth century. At left is the Royal Crescent with its spacious lawn. It is connected by Brock Street to the Circus at the right.

Introduction

ALMOST AS LONG as cities have existed, they have been laid out in some plan so as to provide areas for living, moving about, and working. It is only in fairly recent times that city planning as a term that connotes a formalized body of theory and knowledge has come into general use. What exactly city planning is depends on who is trying to define the phrase. Ask a sociologist, and he will give one answer; ask an economist, he will give another. A philosopher will discuss city planning in terms of his field while an architect will do so in different terms.

The fantastic growth of cities and the problems their growth has raised are so complex that few people seem to agree on solutions. Should we try to cure the cities' ills, or should we let them die while we build new ones? Some thinkers on the subject feel that the population explosion demands new cities, while others contend that new cities will cause the further decay of older cities by draining away their middle-class inhabitants.

It is not the purpose of this book to espouse any special view of city planning or to take a critical position on what has been done, is being done, or what is proposed in the field for the future. It is hoped that the mere raising of issues and a presentation of facts and ideas might serve as inspiration for positive action on the part of readers.

Air pollution.

What's Wrong with Our Cities?

Automobile traffic jams a main artery leading into New York during
the morning rush hour.

Substandard housing.

A hazardous mix of pedestrian and automobile traffic at a busy intersection.

Ugly downtown business street.

Overcrowded recreational facilities.

A city street darkened by the shadow of an elevated transit system.

Residential section engulfed by industry.

Boys playing in littered backyard.

Market day at a village in southern Morocco.

1

A Short History of Cities

Why Do People Live in Cities?

TO DELVE into the history of human settlements is to find not one but several answers to the questions of why people live in cities, and where and how cities grew. According to anthropologists, man is a social animal, instinctively living in groups, as do ants, bees, elephants, wolves, and many other members of the animal world. In Paleolithic times, one family or perhaps several groups moved from place to place, constantly seeking new sources for food — hunting, fishing, or berry-picking sites. The Neolithic period saw the refinement of man's implements, permitting him to plow and to cut trees. Sometime later he also learned to domesticate animals. He no longer needed to roam the forests and plains of the river valleys in search of food, but could raise what he needed by settling in one place.

In fact he found he could produce more than enough to feed himself and his family, and the surplus thus created formed the basis for trade. Division of labor within groups was a result of trade, and groups of craftsmen developed who could transform raw products into commodities that could be bartered for food and other necessities. Spinners, weavers, and dyers of wool, for example, could live together in communities with potters, and tanners of leather.

Division of labor, beneficial to man in many ways, also brought with it a curse that provided us with one of the most serious ills of the city, and plagues us to this day — class structure. At the bottom of the social ladder were slaves or free servants, with craftsmen and tradesmen on a higher rung, and landowners, priests, and rulers placed above them in ascending order. Variations on this pattern existed in different parts of the world, of course, depending on local conditions. In the Western world, the structure became increasingly complex, and finally reached its worst state in the Industrial Revolution of the nineteenth century.

Since farming has always been the source of life's necessities, it was natural that the earliest settlements known grew up in fertile river valleys such as that of the Nile in Egypt, the Tigris–Euphrates in Mesopotamia, the Ganges in India and several valleys in China.

In these settlements, in addition to the groups of craftsmen and tradesmen already mentioned, were added scribes who could keep records of transactions, carpenters, masons, soldiers, and a myriad of others. Villages grew into towns, towns into cities.

Farmers and villagers from the countryside made periodic trips to the city to trade their produce for the articles of the craftsmen. Storehouses for surplus food were built. A rhythm of trade developed, with a certain day of the week devoted to the trading of wool, and another to the trading of camels. Towns that are primarily centers of such trading — market towns — are still common all over Europe, parts of Asia and Africa, and North and South America. Today, such towns traditionally keep a specific day of the week as general market day. Wednesday is market day in Marrakesh, Morocco; Thursday in Lancaster, Pennsylvania; Friday in Verona, Italy.

People living together in large numbers and in close proximity had to provide for themselves a code of behavior, a system of laws. The types of governmental systems differed from region to region depending on how each society had developed. Religion played a chief role in some instances, the need for protection in others. In Egypt, where religion developed very early, the head man of a settlement was also its religious leader, a priest-king. Eventually a number of towns came under the domination of one such man, a Pharaoh. In the Tigris–Euphrates Valley — called the Fertile Crescent — the story was somewhat different. The city of Babylon grew great, not only because of the fertility of the soil, but because of its strategic site at a point where the Tigris and Euphrates Rivers were so close that a canal had been dug connecting them, thus providing water transportation in several directions. Since it was also situated at the crossing of the main land routes to Damascus and the cities of Egypt, Babylon was the envy and the target of tribes from the other sides of the mountains. Protection against them was of prime importance, and was provided by means of high, thick walls. There government developed along military lines, with a king who was also a warlord.

Greece and Rome, which succeeded Egypt and Babylonia as probably the two most important centers of Western civilization, developed still differently.

The Greek city-state was an independent political unit which included both the chief town and surrounding villages and farms. Two unique features of the Greek city were the agora and the acropolis. The agora began as an open space where political meetings were held, and gradually developed into a market area. The acropolis was the religious center, usually consisting of a number of temples, outdoor altars, and statues of deities.

In Roman cities, the forum usually combined the religious and commercial functions of the Greek agora and acropolis. The great Forum Romanum in Rome, however, was solely sacred in character, and smaller forums served as market-places.

Colonies of the Roman Empire, in what is now Italy, France, Germany, Spain, and England, formed the bases of some of the earliest European cities, many of which have survived to the present time. Examples are London, Paris, Naples, Florence, and Cologne.

An artist reconstructed this version of the city of Babylon as it probably looked in the sixth century B.C., having based his conception on descriptions by Herodotus and other Greek historians as well as actual discoveries of archaeologists. The bridge in the foreground connected two parts of the city separated by the Euphrates River.

Where and How Did Cities Grow?

Cities that grew up during the Middle Ages in Europe, like their predecessors in Asia, differed from each other in character depending on their origins and their purposes. Again, the most important factors were economic, social, and religious. Port towns developed where harbors were good or rivers deep enough to permit ships to navigate; market towns where either river or road transportation coincided with centers of agricultural production. The social and economic structure — feudalism — of medieval Europe provided another factor in the form and development of towns. With the emergence of the lord of the manor — the baron — as the one responsible for the protection of his servants, serfs, and usually the free craftsmen and tradesmen too, the castle town arose. Its dominant feature was the heavily walled castle-fortress towering above the huts of the people, which were either huddled at its foot or within its walls.

Another type of medieval settlement was the cathedral town, the seat of the bishop. Hence, much of the life centered about an imposing Romanesque or Gothic edifice which dominated the town and gave it its unique character.

In the Western Hemisphere — in what is now Mexico and Guatemala — although only ruins of great monuments have been found, archaeologists have recently concluded that the Mayan, Aztec, and other peoples of that region had developed sizable cities in prehistoric times. Archaeological exploration will no doubt some day give us clues as to the nature of these cities.

If we look at North American cities and why they grew where they did, we find the same pattern as in the Old World. Baltimore, Boston, Vancouver, and San Francisco grew because of their good harbors; Pittsburgh and St. Louis because of their sites at the confluence of navigable rivers;

Duluth was a natural inland port for the shipping of nearby iron deposits; Charlotte, North Carolina, boasted natural waterpower for the running of mills; while Scranton, Pennsylvania, could use the coal mined nearby in processing the local iron ore.

Other cities have grown, not because of their sites, but because of their purposes. Salt Lake City was founded by a religious sect in an unpromising, desertlike spot, which was literally made to blossom by the Mormons. Brigham Young, the Mormon leader and founder of the city, had the foresight to plan such wide streets that today, over one hundred years later, Salt Lake City has few of the traffic problems that plague most American cities.

Some towns and cities have grown because they were designated as seats of state government: Lincoln, Nebraska, and Boise, Idaho. Still other cities developed as centers of higher education: Ann Arbor, Michigan, and Champaign, Illinois.

Dover Castle, built in A.D. 1180 on the southeast coast of England.
Such a castle, protected by walls and a moat, could serve as a refuge for
the townspeople living in its shadow in times of war.

ench Gothic cathedral at Chartres dominates the city both as its
rchitectural feature and as the center of its religious life.

San Francisco with the Golden Gate Bridge in the foreground. An example of a city sited because of a good natural harbor.

The Form of Cities

Some towns and cities have been laid out according to a definite plan, while others have achieved their form as a result of their natural sites — on a hilltop, or along roads, waterways, or harbors. The layouts of towns and cities fall into four chief types, all of which have countless variations.

The earliest known — and still the most common and most popular — is the gridiron plan. Adapted from Babylonian cities by the Greeks, its popularity probably arises from the fact that it's the simplest and the easiest to lay out. The gridiron plan consists of a pattern of streets crossing each other at right angles, creating square or rectangular plots of land.

When a town has grown up along a road which serves as a main street with cross streets feeding into it, the result is called a spinal or linear plan. Hundreds of towns in the southern, midwestern, and western United States have developed this way. Accidental in most cases, it has been proposed by some contemporary planners as a means of

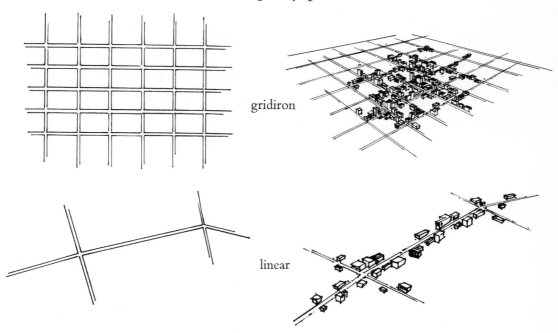

gridiron

linear

Two of the four chief forms of cities as they would look as formal plans (left) and also in perspective as they might appear from an airplane (right).

connecting cities along the Eastern Seaboard of the United States in a planned solution to the megalopolis that already seems to be developing without plan.

Another type of accidental plan is called curvilinear. More informal than any of the others, it has usually resulted from a site where streets followed the natural contour of hills and valleys, or paralleled an irregular shoreline. Many medieval cities, built on hilltops for protection, have variations of the curvilinear plan. It has been used consciously in the United States, to get away from the rigidity of the gridiron plan, and to introduce a quality of informality and relatedness to nature.

Another formal plan is that in which streets radiate from a center and are connected at a number of points by a series of concentric arteries. This radioconcentric plan can be found in towns of the Hittites of 2000 B.C., and in some medieval cities of Europe. It has also been proposed in new plans for Washington, London, and Moscow.

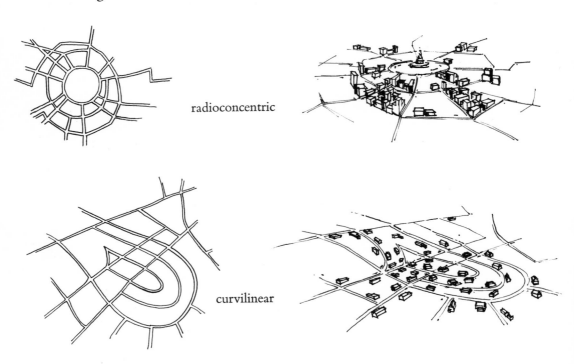

radioconcentric

curvilinear

Two of the four chief forms of cities as they would look as formal plans (left) and also in perspective as they might appear from an airplane (right).

What Has Happened to Cities?

As in the answers to the questions of why people live in cities, or why cities developed where they did, there is no one, single or simple answer to this question. But it must be stated that today's cities are in a state of crisis. The reasons for this crisis are many and interrelated.

First of all, cities are overcrowded. The term *overcrowded* means simply that there are more human beings per square mile than what is conducive to safe, sanitary, and decent living. Overpopulation of cities is the result of several causes: the increase in the birthrate, the decrease in infant mortality, combined with the increase in the longevity of human life — results of strides in modern medicine — and the immigration to the city of people from rural areas.

Because of the overpopulation with its concomitant ills, and the attraction of a more informal and healthier life among trees and grass, thousands of people in middle-income groups have moved to suburban areas. Cities have been left more and more to the wealthy and the poor. The influx of more poor from areas inside and outside the United States into already overcrowded, depressed sections, has created large slum areas.

Although the invention of the automobile has greatly benefited man, its use in greater and greater numbers every year has caused one of the city's most pressing problems. The daily need of thousands of suburbanite commuters to reach the city has caused automobile traffic in and out of many cities that all but strangles them. The increase in automobile traffic has been paralleled by a deterioration in public transit. Commuter rail lines have not only failed to keep up with the population growth, but have decreased their service.

Air pollution is still another of the city's ills. Factories and power plants pour thousands of tons of soot into the city's atmosphere every year. The second-largest polluter of the air is the automobile, whose gasoline engine produces noxious fumes.

Most cities in the United States have grown so rapidly without plan that very few have left enough space for recreational areas. The parks and playgrounds of most cities are either too small for the numbers they serve, or they are located in outlying sections where they are not readily accessible to the people of the inner city.

The last — but hardly the least important — sickness of the American cities — is the way they look, or what might be called the neglect of aesthetic quality. Again, rapid, unplanned growth, the economics of private enterprise, a Puritan heritage which ignored the arts, and the lack of enlightened rulers to whom European cities owe much of their beauty, are some of the reasons behind the ugliness of American cities. Even when government has attempted to sponsor aesthetic improvement in cities, the low level of taste and the politics involved have interfered with any effective improvements.

What Can Be Done to Cure the City's Ills?

In considering all the things that are wrong with cities, it is obvious that the problem of making cities better places in which to live and work are many and complicated. Some planners feel that cities are beyond help, that the only solution is to build new ones. Most thinkers on the subject — economists, sociologists, architects, critics, and city planners — take the position that new life can be infused into existing cities. That it is not necessary to take an either-or position is proved by the fact that plans for the revitalization of cities — plans usually called urban renewal — are being put into effect in many countries while new cities are being designed and constructed at the same time.

Whether cities are to be rebuilt or started from scratch, the same factors must be considered in planning.

LAND USE

In most cities the problem of overcrowding, of congested streets, of scarcity of squares and parks is not the result of too little space, but of poor use of existing space. There is plenty of room for all the component parts that make up the city: homes, stores, office and public buildings, factories, schools, theaters, parks, streets, pedestrian walks, parking facilities, and railroads. Land use is concerned with the way the various components are fitted, like pieces in a puzzle, into the limited number of square miles that comprise the city.

HOUSING

How people are to be housed depends on several factors: family income, best use of available land, and personal choice. In most cities the population density makes high-rise apartments a necessity for all income groups. Sometimes, if space permits, a combination of detached homes, two- or three-story garden apartments, and high-rise apartment buildings can all be built. The *town house* is a solution for those who prefer small houses to apartment living. Town houses are usually semidetached, two-story buildings in rows or clusters. They are a feature of Reston, Virginia, of Chicago's South Side urban renewal, and of Montreal's Nuns' Island.

How people are housed is one problem, but where they live in relation to where they go to school and where they work and play is still another, and equally important, factor in planning. For children to have to go long distances to schools makes no sense. Housewives should be able to shop for groceries in their neighborhoods. People who work should not have to spend long hours getting to and from their jobs. Parks, play areas, and theaters should be easily accessible to families.

CIRCULATION

Not only is it important for people to travel into and out of the city with ease and speed, but it is also necessary for the circulation inside the city to function smoothly. Circulation also includes the moving of goods into and out of the city. Food and the raw materials of industry are two chief items that must be brought in, and the products of a city's factories have to be shipped out. When express highways are built, bringing more and more automobiles and trucks into the city, streets become clogged, sometimes to the point where traffic comes to a standstill. A solution favored by many planners is the increased construction of rail and subway lines or other forms of mass transit, not to replace the automobile, but to supplement it. One solution of the intra-city circulation that has been proposed — and tried on a small scale and in several variations — is a vertical plan, in which express traffic for nonlocal cars, buses, and trucks speeds through tunnels or cuts, local traffic moves at ground level, and pedestrians use overpasses. An attempt to keep some of the heavy trucking out of downtown areas has recently been made by both Paris and New York, by relocating their wholesale food markets from central points to the outskirts.

EDUCATION

The right of every child to have at least an elementary- and secondary-school education is taken for granted in the United States. Yet many cities do not plan either for sufficient school facilities or for easy access to schools. In some cities children must be bussed to their schools; in others children are forced to cross heavily traveled traffic arteries and intersections in getting to school.

RECREATION

Everybody needs some form of relaxation — watching television, playing tennis, painting, or just sitting on a bench in the sun. Cities do have recreational facilities, but in many places they are neither sufficient in number nor conveniently located for the people who use them. Chicago is one of the few cities in the United States that, during its rapid growth in the nineteenth century, set aside both large and small tracts of land in widely diverse sections for the development of parks. New York too had the foresight to block out two huge tracts, in the centers of Manhattan and Brooklyn, as park areas. Although they are beautifully landscaped and offer a rich variety of recreational facilities, including boating, cycling, walking, ball-playing, skating, dining, and listening to music, the New York parks are used by only the relatively few of the city's millions who are fortunate to live near them. Smaller parks, green areas, and playgrounds, within walking distance of the people who use them, should dot the city and supplement the large areas that can offer a greater variety of activities.

AESTHETICS

The old saying that man does not live by bread alone has its implications for city planning. Man has always searched for something more than the material and practical things of life. In every culture peoples have adorned even the trappings of everyday life: their canoe paddles, their eating utensils, their clothing, their homes. To plan cities without considering how they will look is unthinkable. Yet, many times, the economics of construction stand in the way of achieving beauty. That is the argument often used, but it is hardly a valid one. The loss of property taxes that results from setting aside large tracts of the most valuable land in the center of cities for parks, squares, playgrounds, and broad boulevards is a poor excuse for not doing so. It can be done — and has been done, in such cities as Philadelphia, Pittsburgh, Boston, and St. Louis, and is being done in Omaha and New Haven.

Americans traveling abroad are struck by the beauty of many European cities: Paris with its wide, tree-lined boulevards and vistas that give prominence to majestic public buildings; Rome with its many squares featuring statuary or fountains; Amsterdam, Stockholm, Venice, Leningrad — each has its distinctive features of monuments, waterways, spaciousness. Much of the character and beauty of such cities is a result of their gradual growth and a reverence for beauty on the part of their rulers. In some instances — Rotterdam and London — wars and fires have provided opportunities for rebuilding large sections. American cities are relatively new and have grown too fast. What landmarks do exist many times are not respected for their architectural character, and are demolished to make room for more economically

practical or profitable buildings. Only in relatively recent
years have Americans realized the importance of saving their
landmarks. New York is one of the few cities to have established a Landmarks Commission with enough authority to
protect buildings that have either historic or aesthetic interest.

High-rise housing units set far enough apart to provide light, air, and
playground space for children.

Two examples of contemporary rapid transit system. Right: Tokyo's monorail linking the downtown section with the airport. Below: A scene in one of the beautifully designed stations of Montreal's Metro (subway).

Piazza San Pietro (St. Peter's Square) in Rome. A curved colonnade encloses a large space which, with an obelisk and fountains, lends a dramatic setting for the imposing façade of the Basilica of St. Peter.

2

Plans and Planners

To say that a planner has arrived at his ideas on his own, or that his concepts are completely original, would be negating the very essence of history. For every innovator, whatever his field, there are usually people, facts, or events that shape or influence his thinking. When we look at the history of city planning we see this principle at work most of the time.

The man who is probably the most likely candidate for the title of father of city planning is a fifth-century Greek, Hippodamus. Although he is credited with the use of the gridiron plan in designing a number of Greek cities, he probably adopted the idea from the ancient cities of Babylonia. The most notable of the cities to which his name was attached was Miletus, his own native city, which had been destroyed during the war with the Persians and was reconstructed on his plans, which included fifty-two parks and gardens.

Although better known for his painting and architectural ideas than as a planner, Leonardo da Vinci described and drew up plans for an ideal city, and even went so far as to make definite proposals to the Duke of Milan for the replanning of that city. As in some of his other ideas, he was a visionary, a man so far ahead of his time that his planning ideas were never carried out.

L'Enfant and the City of Washington

When the new United States Congress authorized George Washington to choose a site for a new, permanent capital city — the capital had been located, in turn, briefly in Philadelphia, Princeton, Trenton, New York, and Philadelphia again — he chose an area along the Potomac River that he had known well as a boy.

During the winter at Valley Forge, Washington had met a young Frenchman who had come to America as a volunteer soldier in the Continental Army. The young soldier, Pierre Charles L'Enfant, was an artist who after the war became an architect in New York. When word reached him that a new city was to be planned to serve as the nation's capital, he wrote President Washington of his ambition to plan such a city. Although Jefferson, a man of many talents, had drawn up some rough plans of his own, those of L'Enfant were finally accepted by Washington and the Congress.

L'Enfant, whose father had been a portrait painter at the French court, had been brought up at Versailles, the huge palace of the French kings. The magnificent park of Versailles, laid out in the Baroque manner, with great, tree-lined vistas radiating from a central point, with pools, fountains, and statuary, had a profound influence on him and he conceived of the city to be built on the banks of the Potomac in the same grand manner. The plans called for broad avenues radiating from circles planted with grass and trees. Fountains, columns, obelisks, and even a forty-foot cascade of water adjacent to the Capitol itself were included in the magnificent scheme. L'Enfant was not a man to make compromises, and difficulties soon arose which ended in his being dismissed only eighteen months after he had submitted his plans.

Although many of the details of his layouts were never executed, the basic ideas were retained, and the city of Washington, with its spaciousness, its wide, tree-lined boulevards, and its Baroque dignity still reflects the farsighted imagination of L'Enfant.

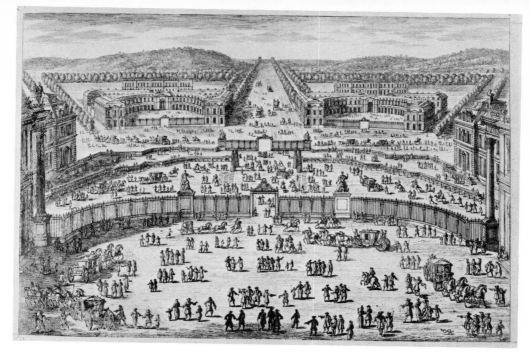

A seventeenth-century engraving of a view of the city of Versailles showing the tree-lined avenues radiating from the palace (foreground). This grand plan was L'Enfant's inspiration for that of Washington.

Ellicott drew this plan of Washington following L'Enfant's original idea. It shows how the Capitol and the President's House were given prominence as the chief features in a radial plan superimposed on a gridiron plan.

Haussmann and the Rebuilding of Paris

Paris — the ancient Roman town of Lutetia — had grown up as a maze of narrow houses and tiny, crooked streets on two islands in the Seine River and along its banks. Surrounded by ramparts, the only place for its teeming population to grow was to spill over beyond the walls. The ramparts were gradually replaced by grand boulevards. This happened three times — in the fourteenth, sixteenth, and seventeenth centuries — so that the plan of the city became a series of boulevards in ever larger concentric circles.

Before the Revolution, a number of French kings had been responsible for beautifying Paris by opening up squares and parks, planting trees, and constructing imposing palaces and bridges over the Seine. Under the reign of Napoleon III in the nineteenth century, a man of vision and courage entered the picture and created the splendid city as it stands today. The man: Baron Georges Eugène Haussmann, a student of law and music who rose very quickly in the French civil service to become the prefect of the Paris district. He planned great new boulevards radiating from circles, new bridges and public buildings, including the famous opera house, designed by the architect Charles Garnier. He widened existing streets, creating magnificent vistas. The most dramatic of these is the boulevard called the Champs-Elysées, a wide, tree-lined avenue that connects the Place de la Concorde and L'Etoile, in the center of which stands the Arc de Triomphe.

Beautification was not Haussmann's only purpose. According to his own stated aims, he was "disencumbering the large public buildings, palaces and barracks in such a way as to make them more pleasing to the eye, afford easier access on days of celebration, and a simplified defence on days of riots."

So costly were his schemes, however, with the money coming out of the taxpayers' pockets, that he was finally dismissed from public office.

An aerial view of Paris with the Arc de Triomphe and the tree-lined
boulevards radiating from it. The Champs-Elysées stretches from an
arch toward the Tuileries Gardens and the Louvre (top center).

41

The Place de la Concorde in Paris, one of Europe's great squares; dominated by a fountain, with the Church of the Madeleine in the background.

Ebenezer Howard and His Garden Cities

During the last quarter of the nineteenth century a young English clerk emigrated to the United States to become a farmer. Failing dismally, he eventually returned to England to pursue a career as a Parliamentary reporter. But Ebenezer Howard was a man of imagination. Experiencing the crowded conditions of the English cities and their effect on people's lives, he decided that something could — and should — be done about the situation. In America he had been inspired by the sight of new villages and towns springing up in the Midwest, and realized that there was still room in England for new towns that would provide better living conditions than the old.

His book, *Garden Cities of Tomorrow*, published in 1902, outlined his ideas. Proposing that city-living and country-living both had assets and limitations for humans, Howard's concept was based on a synthesis of the two. Basing his plan on the number of people who should occupy one acre of land — his figure of ninety to ninety-five is now considered to be too high — he proposed a type of balanced community that would provide housing, greenbelts and parks, industrial areas, farmlands, and the necessary roads and avenues to connect all these sections. His plan — made to be flexible according to the site — consisted of a huge circle, the central core of which was a park. Radiating from the core, a series of broad avenues led to concentric belts, first of residential and shopping areas, then of mills and factories, and finally, of farms. Schools, playgrounds, and still more park areas were included in Howard's plan. Each such garden city, he felt, should house about 30,000 people, with another 2,000 doing the farming.

Since Howard was a practical man, not just a dreamer, and his plan was predicated on feasibility according to current land costs, he was able to interest influential people in politics and business into giving his ideas concrete form. The building of the garden city of Letchworth and later, Welwyn, both on the outskirts of London, was the beginning of a movement that took hold in several European countries and the United States. Howard's book has been credited by Lewis Mumford, the American cultural historian, as having "done more than any other single book to guide the modern towns planning movement . . ."

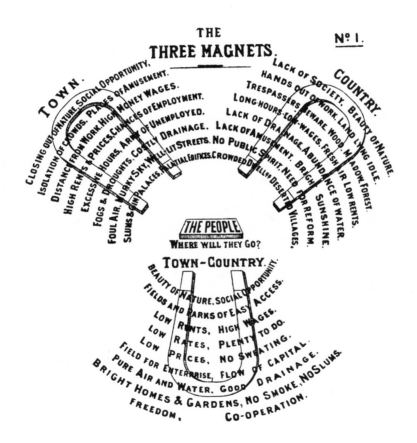

Ebenezer Howard's analysis of the advantages and disadvantages of life both in town and country, and his solution, called *Town-Country*, in which all the advantages are combined.

Howard's diagram of a section of his proposed Garden City. A civic center is surrounded in succession by parklands, residential and shopping areas, industry, and finally, farms.

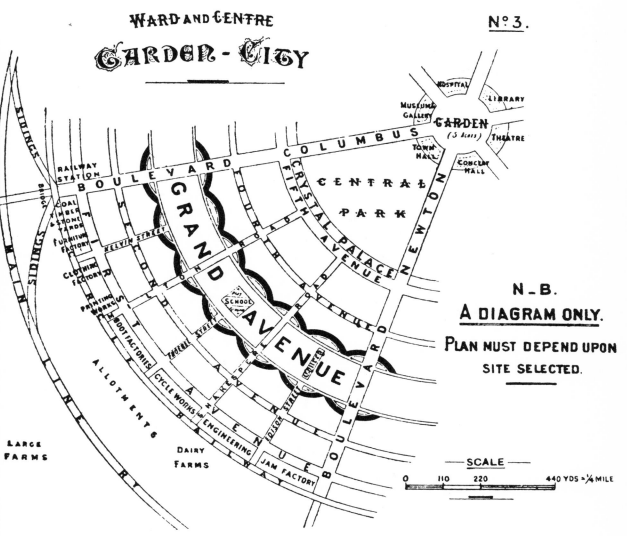

WARD AND CENTRE OF GARDEN CITY

Broadacre City: An Idea of Frank Lloyd Wright

Although Frank Lloyd Wright's fame rests primarily on his great contributions to architecture, he, like Ebenezer Howard, was a man of many ideas. As a social philosopher he maintained that man not only creates his environment, but is, in turn, shaped by that environment. Deeply committed as well to the concepts of democracy, he saw a relationship of man's free exercise of his own will to his physical surroundings and living conditions. Using the word *Usonian* to describe his idea of the ideal community, and *organic* to describe the natural character of man's dwellings, his book *When Democracy Builds* elaborated on his theories. In it he proposed a new type of self-contained community which he called Broadacre City. Based on the premise that man's well-being is in direct relation to his closeness to the earth and to broad, open spaces, Broadacre City consists of a huge, sprawling tract of land. Homes for families of different income levels, a civic center, hospitals, schools, a sports arena, roadside markets, overhead service stations, factories, and farms are all included. Transportation is provided by automobiles of his own design and by helicopter taxis. A few high-rise office and apartment buildings dot the landscape as huge exclamation points. Wright, always thinking in architectural terms, actually designed many of the buildings already mentioned. Broadacre City was never built, and exists only as a series of models and drawings. Many of Wright's ideas, however, have been incorporated into later developments and have become a reality.

Drawing of a detail of Frank Lloyd Wright's Broadacre City. Towering over wheat fields on the right is a high-rise apartment building. Wright conceived and designed helicopter taxies and streamlined automobiles many years before they became a reality.

Le Corbusier: Two Dreams and a Reality

Like Wright, the Swiss-born Charles Edouard Jeanneret, known as Le Corbusier, was primarily an architect, whose ideas about city planning have had a significant impact in several parts of the world. In 1922 he exhibited a model of what he called *Une Ville Contemporaine* (A Contemporary City), which was designed on principles similar to those of Howard and Wright — but with one very important difference. Dividing the main activities of a city into four functions — work, housing, transport, and amenities — his plan called for the construction of high-rise office buildings for work, and also tall apartment houses, in place of Wright's earthbound, family dwelling units for housing. All these tall structures would be, according to this plan, surrounded by large, parklike areas which would allow for plenty of sunlight and air for the inhabitants. Under transport, the plan called for underground rapid transit with direct underground connection to every skyscraper, and elevated highways, leaving ground areas for the most part free of traffic.

Wright's Broadacre City was planned when the automobile was in its infancy, and very few were in use. He did not foresee the thousands of cars which would soon be jamming the roads, taking large tracts of valuable ground space, and making life difficult for pedestrians. Le Corbusier's plan was more realistic, although it, like Wright's, was never built.

His book, *La Ville Radieuse* (*The Radiant City*), published in 1935, included another dream of a vertical garden city, to be used in the expansion of the city of Moscow.

Several of Le Corbusier's plans have materialized, however, in Spain, North Africa, and South America. The most exciting, perhaps, is the city of Chandigarh.

Le Corbusier's plan for a neighborhood of Paris as it appeared in his book *La Ville Radieuse*. Only five percent of the land was to be occupied by buildings. In the center of the drawings is a two-level highway crossing, the first time any such concept had been pictured.

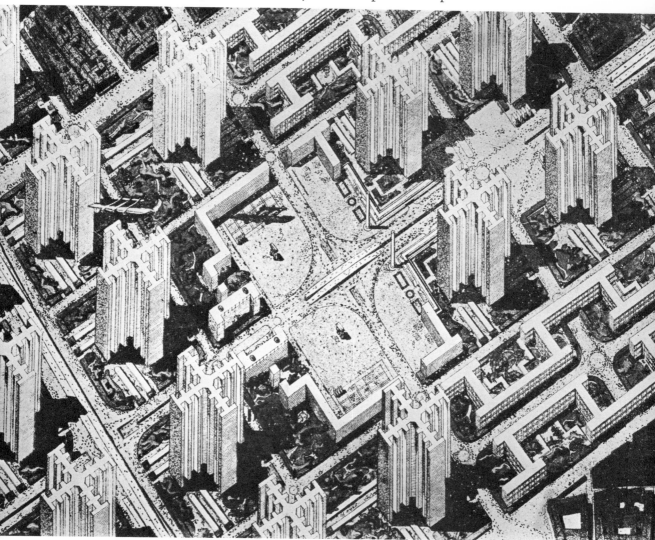

Chandigarh: Le Corbusier's Chance

Tension between the two largest of the many religious groups of India, the Hindus and the Moslems, who had long been at odds, broke into active fighting in 1947, when the British Colonial rule of India came to an end. The fighting stopped with the division of the subcontinent and the creation of two countries — Hindu India, and the largely Moslem state of Pakistan. The new international boundary, however, cut through the former province of Punjab, the capital of which, Lahore, along with the western section of the province, now lay on the Pakistani side of the border. A new seat of government was needed for East Punjab, which remained in India, and no existing town in the state seemed expandable for the purpose. It was India's great, forward-thinking Prime Minister, Jawaharlal Nehru, who envisioned a new city as symbolic of the country's newly found freedom, "unfettered by the tradition of the past."

The very method of choosing the site was in keeping with Nehru's words: airplane reconnaissance. A gently sloping plain within view of the southern Himalayas was decided upon as the location of the new city. Although initial plans were made by others, it was Le Corbusier who was finally approached by Indian government officials to be the master planner and chief architect of the new state capital, Chandigarh.

Almost thirty years after he first revealed to the public his ideas for his Contemporary City, Le Corbusier had the opportunity to put some of them into effect.

Some of his earlier ideas of dividing the city into residential, commercial, educational, and governmental areas were incorporated into the plan for Chandigarh. The most important aspect of the plan, however, was the establishment of neighborhood units or sectors, which were really an extension of the superblocks of Radburn and the Greenbelt towns. Each sector was large enough to support an elementary school, shops, and recreational and cultural facilities. Thus, community life was made possible within the larger boundaries of the city.

Religious rivalries did not end, however, with the establishment of the Moslem state of Pakistan. East Punjab, with its northern half populated by Hindus and its southern half by Sikhs, another religious group, was again divided by the Indian government in 1966. The Hindu part constituted the new state of Haryana. Chandigarh, lying close to the new boundary line, was declared the capital of both states. The Sikhs protested, demanding exclusive possession of the city. Three years later, with violence mounting, a decision was made to award the disputed city to East Punjab. To appease the Hindus a fertile and prosperous piece of territory was carved out of Punjab and handed over to Haryana.

Chandigarh, with miles of streets laid out, but with acres of land still empty of buildings, has a raw, unfinished look which time will hopefully erase.

Chandigarh. Low-cost housing of poured concrete.

Islamabad: A New Capital for a New State

Pakistan, following in the footsteps of India and spurred by the leadership of its president, Mohammed Ayub Khan, decided to symbolize its new statehood by building a new capital. With the city of Karachi serving as the temporary seat of government, work was begun in 1961 on the new capital of Islamabad. As in the case of Chandigarh an outsider was selected both to plan the city and to design most of its buildings. He was a Greek, Constantinos Doxiadis, who had been making an international reputation in the field of city planning. Doxiadis brought into play the human element in his plan, grouping housing units into communities, each with its own shops, elementary school, and mosque. Most of the small individual homes and attached houses are in a style that combines the local traditional elements with modern features. High-rise apartments serve here and there to punctuate the landscape, and impressive governmental buildings will, when completed, provide a focal point for the new city.

Islamabad, like Chandigarh, is far from finished. In 1968 it had a population of 60,000, and by 1980 government officials expect it to house half a million people.

The Secretariat Building designed by Le Corbusier. The raw, unfinished look of the surroundings is typical of the new cities of Chandigarh and Brasilia, and was also characteristic of Washington for many years.

A sprawling residential area of Islamabad, new capital of Pakistan. In the foreground are a mosque and minaret, their traditional style contrasting with the contemporary architecture of the homes.

Brasilia: The Story of a Vision

When Brazil was settled in the sixteenth century, it was both logical and advantageous to establish cities along its Atlantic coast. Good harbors for ships arriving from Europe, a pleasant climate, and fertile soil were positive factors in the settlement of the coastal areas. Transportation to inland areas was extremely difficult and hazardous during pioneer days because of the high mountains and hardly navigable rivers.

But as early as the eighteenth century, visionary Brazilians had set down the principle that the capital of the country — a country larger than the continental United States, excluding Alaska — should be moved inland. The Constitution of 1891 gave the principle a legal framework, but not until 1956 did the actual construction of Brasilia begin.

A contest for a pilot plan for the new capital was held, in which the designs of more than sixty Brazilian architects

Plan of Brasilia. The solid black is an artificial lake.
1. Plaza of Three Powers
2. Ministries
3. Bus Station
4. Embassies
5. University
6. Residential Zone
7. Residential Zone
8. Airport
9. Cemetery
10. Municipal Square
11. Railway Station
12. President's Residence.

were submitted to an international jury. Its choice: a leading Brazilian architect and city planner named Lucio Costa. Rarely in history had a planner been given the opportunity that was afforded Costa — to carve out of a wilderness a new city, a city that could be developed from theory to reality. Another Brazilian, Oscar Niemeyer, was chosen to design the chief government buildings. A disciple of Costa, Niemeyer collaborated closely with him in carrying through many of the planner's ideas.

Much of the original construction equipment and materials were flown in, as were the initial workers. Speed was the key word, and three years after the pilot plan was approved, the new capital of Brazil, although far from completed, was inaugurated. Costa's plan for the city's layout consists of a cross, with one axis on a curve, or arc, so that the design resembles an airplane. The tip of the "plane" points to the center of the huge artificial lake that surrounds most of the city. The government buildings form a central core of the plan, closely flanked by a cultural center, banking and shopping centers, and hotels. Residential areas fan out along the great curved axis of the cross, and industrial areas lie still farther away from the center.

The main highway runs directly into the center of the city, elevated and separated by parklike areas so that noise and air pollution from traffic are at a minimum. The flow of traffic is then led into the main districts by means of cloverleaves and secondary roads. Residential areas are arranged in super-blocks, each housing 3,000 people, and each with its own schools and stores.

Time will have to give Brasilia qualities that it may still, in its newness, lack — a cultural life of its own, and a lived-in look that can spell the difference between a handsome shell and a human organism.

The government center of Brasilia on the Plaza of Three Powers,
(1) in the plan. The dome at the left and the saucerlike shape at the
right contain the two houses of the legislature while the twin shafts
between them house the administrative offices.

Brasilia apartment buildings with play area for small children in the
foreground.

3

The New Town Movement around the World

ALTHOUGH EBENEZER HOWARD'S IDEAS created little stir during his lifetime, they have since become the basis for new town planning in various parts of the world. Starting in the United States in the late 1920's a new town movement created Radburn, New Jersey, and the Greenbelt towns of Maryland, Ohio, and Wisconsin. Government policy in Great Britain gave rise to the construction of some thirty new towns beginning in 1946. Hilversum in Holland, Tapiola in Finland, and satellite communities of Frankfort-am-Main in Germany and of Stockholm in Sweden have sprung up. Canada has Nuns' Island in the St. Lawrence River near Montreal, and Kitimat, British Columbia. Reston, Virginia; Columbia, Maryland; and Foster City, California, are in the building stages, while plans for a satellite city across the river from Anchorage, Alaska, have recently been announced. Although most of these new cities have been planned using Howard's basic theories, changes have been the inevitable result of time and place. The increased use of the automobile since Howard's time has necessitated new solutions to the circulation problem. Differing features of landscape and climate, and advances in architecture and engineering have caused many variations on his theme. But the theme is still basically the same: that a city's housing, work, education, recreation, and circulation must be planned as part of a carefully integrated whole to provide the good life for its residents.

New Towns in the United States

Inspired by the thinking and the work of Howard and Unwin in England, a group of American planners and businessmen organized, in the 1920's, the Regional Planning Association of America. Among them were Lewis Mumford, writer and critic; Clarence Stein, architect and planner; and Henry Wright, planner. At about the same time, Stein was appointed chairman of the newly created Commission of Housing and Regional Planning of New York State.

A housing development in the New York City borough of Queens was the first result of the collaboration of Stein with a private developer. Called Sunnyside Gardens, the project provided moderate-cost housing in two-story garden apartments surrounding tree-planted, grassy areas, but contained within the usual gridiron of city blocks.

Successful in the one venture, Stein and Wright went on to create the new town of Radburn on New Jersey farmland only sixteen miles from New York City. Superblocks were the basis of the Radburn plan. Each superblock consisted of a number of house groupings fed by dead-end lanes or culs-de-sac, thus avoiding through automobile traffic. Every superblock also contained a spine of shared parkland. Other unique features at Radburn were the construction of roads for specialized uses, almost complete separation of pedestrian and automobile, and miles of paths with underpasses to keep schoolbound children from having to cross streets.

Radburn never achieved the full status of its English predecessor, Garden Cities, however. The severe economic slump of the period was to blame for its failure to attract its own industry and for the lack of a greenbelt surrounding it. But it was a first step in creating better places to live on this side of the Atlantic.

Plan of the residential districts of Radburn. A centrally located elementary school is connected by paved walkways (the heavy black lines) to all parts of the community.

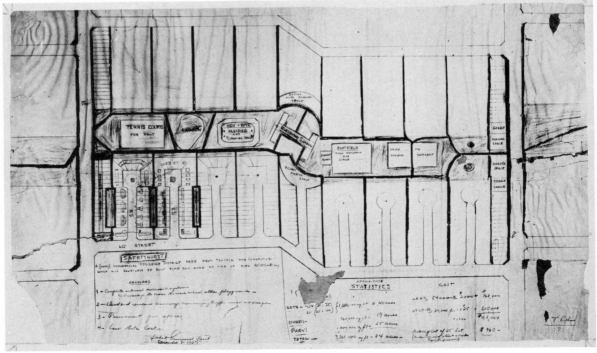

Original sketch plan by Herbert Emmerich for a superblock he called Safetyhurst, with culs-de-sac and a spine of shared land including recreational and educational facilities. The idea eventually became the basis of the Radburn Plan.

Radburn also served as a model when the federal government, during the Roosevelt administration, took the initiative in sponsoring the three Greenbelt towns. Basically the same in concept, and again more suburban in character than the self-sufficient Garden City was to have been, they were Greenbelt, Maryland, just outside Washington; Greenhills, near Cincinnati; and Greendale, near Milwaukee.

Aerial view of Greenbelt, Maryland. The shape of the ridge on which it was built gives it a curvilinear form. At the left center is the town center with a school, shopping center, parking space, and swimming pool.

Reston and Columbia: Cities in Parks

Eighteen miles west of Washington, D.C., lies a beautiful, hilly tract of woods and meadows that is being transformed into the planned city of Reston. To consist of seven villages with an eventual population of 70,000, Reston also includes an industrial zone which will provide jobs for most of its residents. Reston is the idea of Robert E. Simon, a financier and developer with imagination and vision, who brought in planning consultants and architects. The firm of Whittlesey, Conklin, and Rossant is responsible for the master plan.

Each of Reston's villages consists of high- and low-rise apartment buildings, town houses, and individual homes, grouped in clusters. Instead of the usual plot of land for each family, so common to suburban developments, the cluster idea leaves the major part of the woods and meadows untouched for the use of all residents. Each village, too, has a commercial hub which can be reached by pedestrian paths as well as by road. Besides ample shopping facilities the village center includes elementary and nursery schools, library, churches, restaurants, and cafés. Lakes, streams, golf courses and tennis courts, bicycle paths, and walks provide outdoor recreation. Underpasses and footbridges permit children to walk to school without having to cross streets.

Similar to Reston, but planned to be larger, is the city of Columbia, situated in the rolling countryside of Maryland, not far from Baltimore. Also the creation of one man, James W. Rouse, Columbia expects to have a population of 110,000 by 1980.

Several neighborhood units of 700 to 1,000 families will constitute a village. Neighborhoods will have elementary schools, day-care centers, parks, and playgrounds. Village centers will have shopping centers, libraries, community buildings, and high schools. A concert pavilion and theater have already been built, and a large downtown center with stores, restaurants, and nightclubs is in the planning stage. Provisions for the higher education of Columbia's youth include art and music schools, senior and junior colleges. A unique feature is a religious facilities building where Protestants, Roman Catholics, and Jews will worship under one roof.

In Reston and Columbia, some of Ebenezer Howard's principles have finally been realized. In both cities people can live, work, and play in an environment that has been planned to eliminate many of the city's ills.

Town houses and apartments in Lake Anne Village, the first of seven planned village centers in Reston, Virginia. At far right is the commercial center with a church, library, doctors' and dentists' offices, shops, post office and community center.

Cumbernauld: One of Britain's New Towns

The 1940's in Great Britain saw the beginning of a new towns movement that had, by 1968, resulted in thirty such communities. With the passage of the New Towns Act of 1946 the government set the machinery in motion for the formation of development corporations and the necessary funding to build new towns in England, Wales, Scotland, and Northern Ireland. Most of them are satellite towns — towns designed to take overspill from such large cities as London, Birmingham, Liverpool, and Glasgow.

Cumbernauld is one of the Scottish new towns near Glasgow. As one of the latest to be built it has been able to benefit from mistakes made in some of the earlier new towns. It was the first of the new towns planned to cater to a high level (140 percent) of car ownership with appropriate garage and parking facilities. Cumbernauld has also gone farthest in separating automobile and pedestrian traffic, a feature that has made it the safest town in Britain.

Cumbernauld New Town near Glasgow. When this photograph was taken the town center seen at the top of the picture was unfinished. The highway system, with two-level interchanges, ensures steady traffic flow while limiting automobile access to the residential areas.

Tapiola: Garden City of Finland

Rising amid the tall firs and birches near Finland's capital, Helsinki, is the planned and self-contained city of Tapiola. To create and finance it, a number of labor unions and veterans' organizations banded together in 1951 and founded the Housing Foundation Asuntosäätiö as a private, nonprofit enterprise. The foundation was not only responsible for the financing and construction of Tapiola's homes, offices, and industrial plants, but also for streets, water supply, street lighting, parks, gardens, and a power plant. A competition for the design of a city center was won by the Finnish architect Aarne Ervi. Beautifully landscaped, the center boasts a central administrative tower — the landmark of Tapiola — and a large, covered shopping center with a young people's cafeteria and discothèque. Across a reflecting pool are a health center with doctors' offices, clinics, and laboratories, an indoor swimming pool, and a sports hall. A hotel, with convention facilities, a theater-concert hall, and an exhibition hall for fine arts will soon make the city center complete.

A unique aspect of Tapiola is its housing. Amost eighty percent of its sites are allocated to state-subsidized housing for people of low income. High-rise apartment buildings, row houses, and one-family houses are mixed so as to give variety to the living areas. The natural beauty of the site has not only been preserved but has been enhanced with flower plantings and fountains.

Although it has some light industry, Tapiola is not completely self-sufficient economically. Only fifteen minutes by bus or car from the center of Helsinki, its residents can easily commute to work in the capital.

Tapiola, satellite city of Helsinki, Finland. Above: the town center with office building, shopping plaza, parking, gardens, and pool.

Below: mixed-income housing in a beautiful forest setting.

Nuns' Island: Montreal's New City

Since the 1700's a wooded island of 980 acres in the St. Lawrence River belonged to the Sisters of the Congregation of Notre Dame, who had built there a rambling brick building as a retreat. Sold by the order in 1956, Nuns' Island, as it is now called, is rapidly being developed into what might be called a satellite city. Bernard Weissbourd, head of Metropolitan Structures, its builder, maintains that a new town so close to a large metropolitan area — it is only six minutes from downtown Montreal — does not need economic self-sufficiency. As at Tapiola, an industrial park is part of the plan, but will probably not provide enough jobs for all the residents.

Housing is in garden apartments, town houses and high-rise buildings, with the last designed by the famous architect Mies van der Rohe. Each residential area contains a small shopping–community center, with tennis courts and swimming pools. A cul–de–sac in each group of apartments within the neighborhood eliminates through traffic, protecting children at play.

Sections of the island have been set aside for a business and town center, and cultural and recreational facilities, as at Reston and Columbia and other new cities. A huge round barn, one of the early structures on the island, is being preserved for use as a summer theater. To take advantage of its natural setting as an island, marinas for boating will be featured on Nuns' Island.

Above: Nuns' Island in the St. Lawrence River, with Montreal in the background. Below: Model of the residential area shown above, with high- and low-rise apartment buildings and clusters of town houses grouped around cul-de-sac street access and shared green areas. At the left is a community center with an elementary school, supermarket, community building, and swimming pool.

A drawing for the projected improvement of the City Hall area of Philadelphia.

4

Putting New Life into
Old Cities

BEFORE MAN REALIZED that the revitalizing of cities was a dire
necessity if they were to survive and function — a concept
long overdue — the need to rebuild was sometimes forced on
him by the destruction caused by wars and fires. After
London's partial destruction in the great fire of 1666, the
famous architect, Sir Christopher Wren, submitted a plan
for the rebuilding of the burned-out area. Unfortunately,
Wren's plan, which would have changed the largely medieval
aspect of its narrow streets and cramped quarters into a grand
design in the Baroque manner, was never accepted. Fought
by landowners who resisted any change in the boundaries of
their holdings, it was rejected by the king.

San Francisco and Tokyo largely suffered the same fate
when earthquakes and fires leveled great expanses of both.
They too were rebuilt without much regard for imaginative
improvement or a look to the future.

When most of Rotterdam's business section was flattened
by bombs during World War II, however, the opportunity
to build something better than had existed was seized upon
by a forward-thinking municipal government. Coventry in
England and Dresden in Germany, also with severely bombed
business districts, were rebuilt along plans similar to those
used in Rotterdam.

Rotterdam

The bombing of Rotterdam during World War II almost totally destroyed its downtown business district. Instead of having it rebuilt exactly as it had been, the city fathers saw the wonderful opportunity for a fresh approach to its design. In Dr. C. van Traa they found a man with an imaginative approach. He created, as the main feature of the newly constructed area, a magnificent shopping mall, the Lijnbaan. Lined with two-story shops, which give it a human scale, the mall features colorful flower plantings, shrubs and trees, sculpture, and handsome lighting fixtures. Shoppers can stroll leisurely in these pleasant surroundings, or relax comfortably on its many benches.

The Lijnbaan in Rotterdam's downtown business district, completely rebuilt after its total destruction during World War II bombing raids. Pedestrian shopping mall features flower plantings and sculpture.

Urban Renewal: U.S.A.

Urban renewal in the United States has usually resulted from the work of visionaries with the ability to pull together the various political and business interests of a city. Such men as Edmund N. Bacon in Philadelphia, Richard C. Lee in New Haven, Alden Aust in Omaha, and Edward Logue in Boston not only have had the ideas but also the personal dynamism and administrative ability to see the ideas carried out.

Great impetus was given to the movement with the passing of the Federal Housing Act of 1949. Under its terms, federal subsidies were made available to cities and towns to build low- and middle-income housing on a large scale. Many states and municipal governments have followed suit. But experts and financial support cannot do the necessary revitalization alone. The people who are directly affected must be consulted before plans are approved. To this end community action groups are playing a larger role in planning for urban renewal.

In the forefront of urban renewal in the United States are the cities of Boston, Chicago, Cincinnati, Cleveland, Hartford, New Haven, Omaha, Philadelphia, Pittsburgh, Providence, Rochester, and St. Louis. The story of what has happened in a few of these cities is told in the following pages.

PHILADELPHIA

When William Penn chose the site for the city of Philadelphia in the 1680's he became one of the first city planners in this country. The original city, a tiny fraction of what is today the fourth-largest city in the United States, was located on flat land lying between the Delaware and the Schuylkill Rivers. Using the gridiron plan, Penn had the two-square-mile rectangle divided into four smaller divisions, or quadrants, created by two broad avenues, one — Market Street — running from river to river, and the other — Broad Street — bisecting it at right angles. Where the two streets crossed, he set aside a large parcel of land to be used for public buildings — now the site of City Hall. Park squares were centered in each of the four quadrants, and they still continue to be green oases in the crowded city of today.

Philadelphia overflowed its original boundaries in the

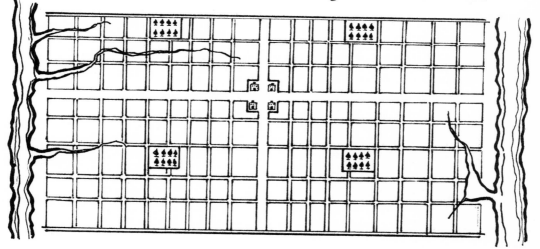

The gridiron plan of Philadelphia as drawn in 1682 showing its location between the Schuylkill River at the left and the Delaware on the right. The wide street running between the two rivers is Market; bisecting it is Broad. The rectangles with the trees represent the parks that William Penn had the foresight to put into the plan, and which, almost three-hundred years later, still provide green oases in the teeming city.

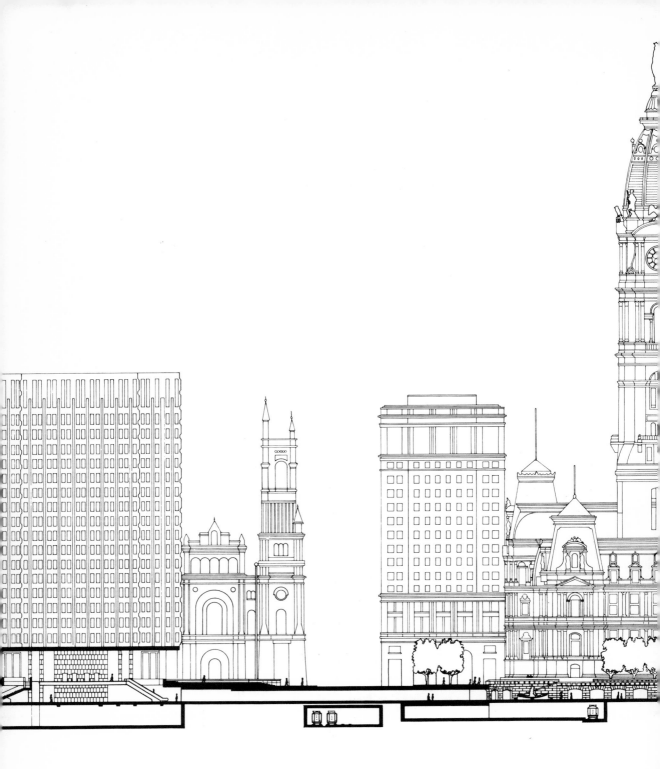

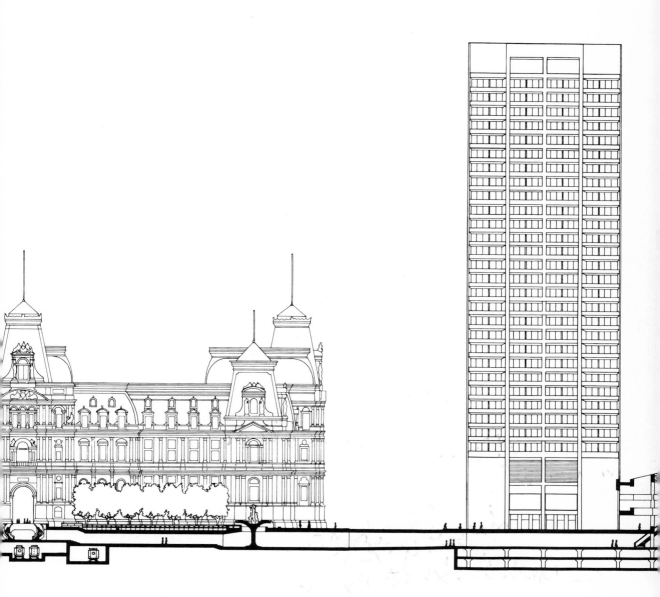

The line drawing above shows the nineteenth-century City Hall
topped by a statue of William Penn and flanked by new office
buildings, some not yet completed. The tall structure immediately to
the right of City Hall is to be built at the end of a sunken mall, as
shown in the drawing on page 70. Details of underground pedestrian
areas are shown in the drawings on page 79.

nineteenth century, and as happened to many another city, became the victim of overcrowding and decay. When the Pennsylvania Railroad built its tracks on an elevated wall running right into the center of the city, another victory was won by men more interested in furthering their commercial interests than in making the city livable.

Philadelphia had not only been the first capital of the thirteen colonies and the temporary capital of the newly proclaimed United States, but also Boston's rival as a social, cultural, and political center. One of its most beautiful buildings was the State House of what was then the Province of Pennsylvania. It was in this handsome, red-brick Georgian building that the Second Continental Congress met and voted the Declaration of Independence in 1776. Independence Hall, as it is called today, stood in a small park which was gradually engulfed in the nineteenth century by office buildings, dingy warehouses, and factories.

Not very far away, Society Hill, one of the oldest residential sections of Philadelphia, and filled with hundreds of beautiful, small, Georgian residences and churches, also met the same fate. Some of the homes were converted to rooming houses and apartments, and others were torn down by commercial interests to make room for warehouses and stores.

What happened to the once gracious city of Philadelphia was no different from what happened to many other American cities. But in the 1950's forward-looking leaders began to turn the tide. With one of the first comprehensive plans, mandated by law and piloted by the courageous executive director of its city planning commission, Edmund N. Bacon, Philadelphia embarked on a number of projects that have put the city in the forefront of urban renewal and made it a pattern for other cities to follow.

The site of the old railroad tracks and station has been transformed into the Penn Center. A complex of high-rise

Drawings for the projected improvement of the City Hall area of
Philadelphia.

office buildings, bi-level shopping arcades, and open garden courts, Penn Center has brought much business, vitality, and beauty back to the center of the city.

In the area surrounding Independence Hall another transformation took place. The decrepit tenements, warehouses, and factories were torn down and replaced by a tree-lined mall at the head of which, architecturally imposing, stands the "cradle of liberty."

The houses of Society Hill are gradually being restored by private funds. An architectural competition to enhance the area was won by I. M. Pei, who not only sited and designed three huge, slablike apartment houses, but created two-story town houses in the area. Although they are in the contemporary style, their scale and materials relate them well to the restored Georgian houses that surround them.

In the Center City, Market East, the latest of Philadelphia's projects is taking shape. Eight blocks long, it will link, in one gigantic terminal, facilities for the Reading and Penn–Central's commuter trains, the subway, a bus depot, and a parking garage for three thousand cars.

The revitalization of Philadelphia has not been an easy task. Federal, state, city, and private moneys have gone into its renewal, and hundreds of community leaders and private citizens have been involved.

Architect's drawing showing Philadelphia's planned Market East project in cross section. Trains, buses, and automobiles are separated at different levels with connecting escalators. The City Hall tower can be seen in the background.

western Pennsylvania, two rivers, the Allegheny and the Monongahela, join to form a third, the Ohio. In the eighteenth century, when it was easier to move goods from one part of the country to another by water rather than by the rough and wooded land routes, such a point was a natural one for a trading post. The "Point," as it was called then, was the scene of bloody battles, with the French, the Indians, and the British all claiming it. Called Fort Duquesne by the French, Fort Pitt by the British, and finally Pittsburgh, its advantageous position combined with the nearby natural gas deposits to make it a center of glass manufacture. Later, with the perfecting of the Bessemer process of steel making, and the proximity of rich iron and coal deposits, its fame as a steel-manufacturing center grew. So did its fame as the "Smoky City."

The point of land formed by the confluence of the rivers was gradually filled with ugly warehouses and factories, which in recent times have become shabby and run-down. To add to the ills of smoke and grimy buildings, the rivers tend to flood their banks during spring thaws, often filling the downtown section with mud.

Together the city and state marshaled their forces in a multi-pronged attack that has completely transformed the blighted area. Army engineers were brought in to build ten dams upstream, controlling the floods. The state announced plans to create a thirty-six-acre park at the "Point," and new smoke regulations were passed, cutting smoke and smog by eighty-eight percent by 1955. The city used its rights to condemn property, and proceeded to sell it to private developers. The result is a complex of high-rise office and apartment buildings called the Gateway Center. In twenty years a decaying section of a great city has been made into the Golden Triangle, and is considered a national model of a revitalization program.

Pittsburgh at the confluence of the Allegheny (left) and the Monongahela (right) rivers. Above: in 1950 before renewal began. Below: an artist's sketch of how the Golden Triangle will appear when completed.

OMAHA

Omaha, named for an Indian tribe of the region, was one of those cities that started as a trading post on a great river, the Missouri. As cattle raising and meat packing gradually became chief industries of the midwestern United States, Omaha became one of their centers.

South Omaha got its start in 1883 when a land syndicate was formed for the purpose of establishing a livestock market. Stockyards and packinghouses sprang up quickly with business blocks and residential areas following in what was a real boom. By 1900 South Omaha, still a separate city, boasted a population of 26,000, with its stockyards and packing plants second only to those of Chicago.

But the trend was reversed in the 1920's and 1930's, the area having long since become part of the city of Omaha. Decentralization of the industry, a result of the advent of long-haul trucking and mechanical refrigeration, and a parallel to such other changes as the growth of outlying industrial parks, shopping centers, and motels, gradually led to South Omaha's economic decline. In 1964 a group of local businessmen, realizing that all was not well, met and decided that something must be done. To finance a study, they raised money and persuaded the city council to match it.

The study itself was a wonderful exercise — one that could well be imitated by other cities — in the coordination of several agencies. The locally led, private Real Estate Research Corporation dealt with the economic portion, the city's Traffic Engineering Division of the Public Works Department tackled the problem of circulation, and the Planning Department, under the leadership of its able director, Alden Aust, undertook the aspects of land use and urban design.

Calling for a refashioning of South Omaha into a shopping center core, the final plan features a pedestrian shopping mall and an entertainment center of restaurants, shops, theater, and bars. With the new John F. Kennedy Expressway skirting the area and feeding traffic into its streets, a pattern of traffic flow has been carefully worked out. Free parking on a large scale is also an important feature — a necessity in our car-oriented age, if such a plan is to work.

South Omaha as it looks today: a sprawling mix of meat-packing plants, small businesses, houses, and parking lots.

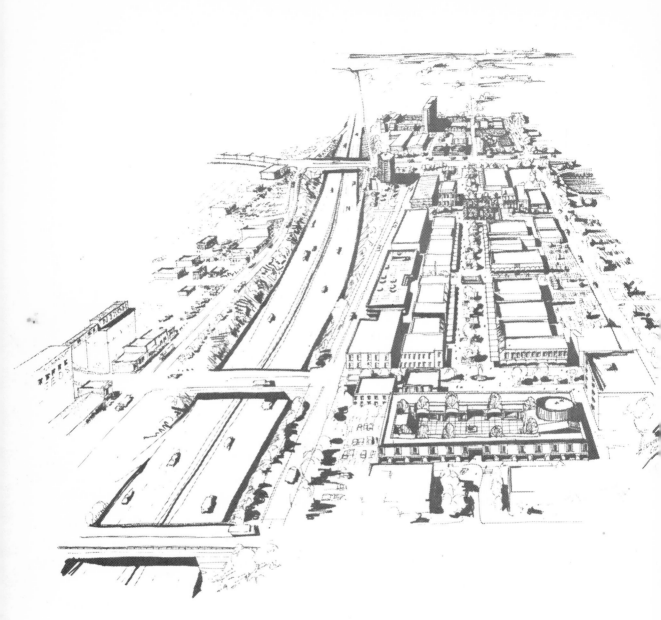

An artist's conception of how South Omaha will appear after its revitalization. The high-rise apartment in the distance is the same one that appears in the aerial photograph at the lower right. A pedestrian shopping mall would replace the wide street in the center of the photograph on page 85. In the foregound is a recreation center.

NEW YORK'S BATTERY PARK CITY

New York City is embarking on an ambitious project that will add ninety-one acres of land to the southern tip of Manhattan Island. By filling in a section of the Hudson River adjacent to the Battery Park and Wall Street areas, space will be provided for a huge project that will change the whole life of the downtown area. Almost four-fifths of the area will be devoted to housing for every income level. One third of the approximately 14,000 apartments are to be low-income, one third middle-income, and one third high-income units.

Unique aspects of the project are its financing and its housing mixture. Subsidized by both government and private funds, the housing units will be thoroughly mixed to create an economically and racially integrated community without enclaves of high- or low-rent housing.

Offices, shops, schools, police and fire stations, a health center, library, and facilities for indoor cultural and recreational purposes will all be included in the project. One of the features that will enhance the area is a plaza and mall connecting most of the buildings at the pedestrian level. With transparent covering and controlled climate it will provide protection from the elements while at the same time permitting sunlight to filter through. Also unusual in the planning of Battery Park City is a zoning resolution which specifies that at least thirty percent of the total site is to be left open for public use. These areas will include plazas, greens, coves, and a magnificent esplanade along the riverfront.

New York's projected Battery Park City. Office and apartment towers contrast with low-rise housing and a spacious esplanade along the Hudson River. River views are stressed in the planning.

A climate-controlled plaza with transparent covering which will permit pedestrians to shop and dine in comfort. A suspended monorail (right center) may serve as a connecting link to other parts of Lower Manhattan.

5

Ideas for the Future

Seward's Success: Climate Control in Alaska

The recent discovery of enormous oil and natural gas reserves in Alaska portends a huge population explosion in the northland in a very short time. To develop the oil and gas fields, to man the various branches of the industry, including refining and transport of the products, and to administer those branches, Alaska will need thousands of people in the near future.

The city of Anchorage, expected to be the industry's base of operation, has already grown rapidly — from 33,060 in 1960 to 115,000 in 1970 — with experts predicting 500,000 by 1980. Foreseeing the need, an imaginative Oklahoma firm, Tandy Industries, has announced plans to build the satellite city of Seward's Success two miles from downtown Anchorage. To be situated in virgin forest country opposite Anchorage across Knik Arm, an inlet of the Gulf of Alaska, Seward's Success will be the world's first climate-controlled city.

Conceived as the future administrative center of the booming industry, the new city will have a population of 20,000. Offices, shops, schools, churches, a sports arena, and hotels will serve the new residents.

One of the most serious obstacles in attracting qualified people to the northland is, of course, the climate. With a mean annual temperature of 36° (minimum in winter, 1°; maximum in summer, 66°), one can readily imagine the reluctance of many to live there.

Climate control is therefore an important aspect in the future success of the project. To achieve it all buildings will be connected with temperature-controlled malls. No coats or boots will have to be worn — except to go to Anchorage, or beyond the limits of the city for winter sports.

To go back and forth to Anchorage, people will ride in a high-speed aerial tramway. Arriving in the new city, they will transfer from the gondola to pedestrian walks and moving sidewalks. Later, as the community grows, a monorail will be built, encircling the city and connecting it with both Anchorage and the International Airport.

An artist's sketch of Seward's Success, satellite city of Anchorage, Alaska. The aerial tramway in the foreground will carry people across Knik Arm, an inlet of the Gulf of Alaska.

The Domed City: Fuller's Dream

One of the most exciting ideas for controlling the atmosphere over cities is that of the architect-engineer R. Buckminster Fuller. Fuller's geodesic domes have already been used for many purposes, including homes, factories, office buildings, and botanical gardens. Probably his best-known structure was the United States Pavilion at the 1967 World's Fair in Montreal, which has been converted into a permanent display of gardens and aviaries.

Fuller contends that his domed city is a workable concept that would control air and water pollution as well as temperature. In northern climates the surface of the dome would be heated by means of electrical resistance wires bedded in the skin, thus melting snow. Water, both from rain and melting snow, would run off into gutters and its flow directed into reservoirs. A dome placed over part of New York, as shown in the photograph, could be paid for in ten years by the saving in the cost of snow removal. Electrical heat for the city would be generated at great distances from the city where pollution from the burning of coal or oil would be disbursed over sparsely populated areas.

All parts of the dome through which sun did not shine directly would be transparent. In summer, polarized glass in those parts of the dome receiving the sun's direct rays would protect the covered area from overheating. Under the dome, people could keep their windows open the year round, and gardens and outdoor restaurants would thrive in the dirt-free air.

Fuller's dream may sound like science fiction now, but we could have said the same thing about man's walking on the moon fifty years ago.

An aerial view of Manhattan Island with Fuller's dome as it would appear if installed over the midtown area. Such a dome would be one mile high at its center.

Stratasystem: A Plan for Tomorrow

When Frank Lloyd Wright and Le Corbusier dreamed their dreams of better places for people to live and work they were thinking of new cities rather than the rebuilding of old ones. A new dream has been dreamed by the New York architectural firm of Eggers and Higgins that should revolutionize the whole field of urban renewal if it can ever be realized.

Approaching the problem with scientific care, a team of the firm's architects have arrived at a solution based on both a social philosophy and the technological skills of our times. With the idea that the family unit and the neighborhood are all-important in our society, they propose that slum areas be renewed without relocating the people who live in them. By building the first housing units of the project on vacant lots and then tearing down the old, deteriorating houses, the usual practice of moving people away from their neighborhood could be avoided.

The concept is based on a series of levels, or strata — from which comes the name Stratasystem. The two lower levels would provide space for parking, police and fire stations, loading and warehousing facilities. On the third level would be support facilities: schools, playgrounds, clinics, clubs, day-care centers, religious and recreational centers, and some office space.

A fourth level would carry all utilities — gas, electricity, water — and, possibly, automated systems for distributing mail and laundry, and moving sidewalks. Above the mechanical level would be a concourse, a pedestrianway connecting all areas of the community. Landscaping, resting areas and small playgrounds would create a social center substituting for the old city block. Small shops and markets would be located in the first level of the apartment buildings which rise from the concourse.

Through an increase in population density by building upward, large amounts of land would be released for parks and waterfront recreational areas and district centers. Flexibility in construction is stressed by the architects, to preserve landmarks and natural features, and to meet the needs of the community.

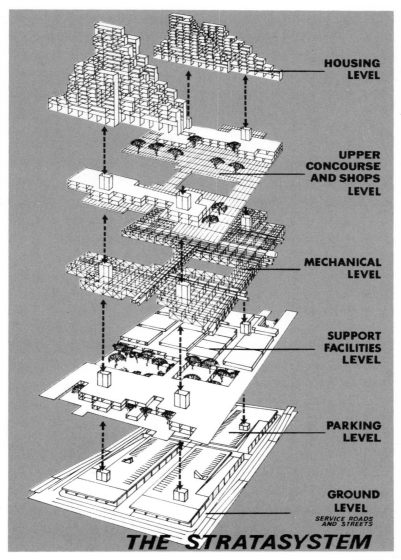

HOUSING LEVEL

UPPER CONCOURSE AND SHOPS LEVEL

MECHANICAL LEVEL

SUPPORT FACILITIES LEVEL

PARKING LEVEL

GROUND LEVEL
SERVICE ROADS AND STREETS

THE STRATASYSTEM

Exploded diagram of Stratasystem with various levels. Arrows show vertical transportation cores for elevators and stairs.

Model of Stratasystem, showing an area of eight self-contained neighborhoods housing 35,200 residents. Housing is provided chiefly in high-rise buildings of varying designs.

Glossary

ACROPOLIS. The fortified upper part of an ancient Greek city. The most famous was that in Athens, which was the religious center and the site of the temple called the Parthenon.

AGORA. Originally the marketplace of ancient Greek cities; it served also as a meeting place for political assembly.

AVIARY. A large enclosure where birds are kept.

BAROQUE. A style of European art and architecture of the seventeenth and eighteenth centuries. In city planning the word refers to an open, formalized layout of streets radiating from squares and circles.

BOULEVARD. A broad street usually lined with trees and grass plots.

CIRCUS. An open circle, square, or plaza where several streets converge.

CONCENTRIC CIRCLES. Circles of different diameters having a common center.

CUL-DE-SAC. A street or lane with one end closed; a blind alley.

CURVILINEAR. Consisting of, or enclosed by curved lines.

EKISTICS. The science of human settlements that concerns the inter-relationships of man with his environment. A word coined by Constantinos Doxiades.

FAÇADE. The front of a building.

GEODESIC. Pertaining to a system of higher mathematics used in dome construction in which the tetrahedron is the basic geometric form.

GEORGIAN. An architectural style developed during the reigns of Queen Anne and the four Georges, 1702–1830; the English adaptation of Baroque.

GRIDIRON. In city planning a pattern of streets crossing each other at right angles, creating square or rectangular plots of land. Sometimes used in the shortened form: grid.

HIGH-RISE. An apartment or office building with a large number of stories.

HITTITES. An ancient people who established a powerful empire in Asia Minor from about 1900 to 1200 B.C.

LINEAR. Arranged in a line. A linear town plan usually consists of one long main street crossed by shorter streets.

LOW RISE. Describing a building with usually one to four stories.

MALL. A wide public walkway usually lined with trees and shrubbery.

MEGALOPOLIS. Several large cities and suburbs which adjoin to form one huge urban area. From Greek words *mega* (large) and *polis* (city).

METROPOLIS. A large city. From the Greek words *meter* (mother) and *polis* (city).

MINARET. A slender tower attached to a mosque.

MONORAIL. A railroad with its cars balanced on, or suspended from, a single rail.

MOSQUE. A Moslem temple or place of worship.

NEOLITHIC. Describing the later part of the Stone Age during which man developed polished stone tools and began to raise cattle. From the Greek words *neos* (new) and *lithos* (stone).

OBELISK. A tapering, four-sided shaft of stone used as a monument.

ORGANIC. As used by Frank Lloyd Wright, a structure that perfectly fulfills its functional requirements.

PALEOLITHIC. Pertaining to the earlier part of the period during which man used stone tools and weapons. From the Greek words *palaios* (old) and *lithos* (stone).

PREFECT. The chief administrative official of a department of France.

PREHISTORIC. Pertaining to the period before man started to record his history.

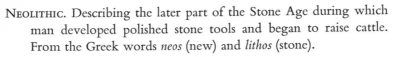

QUADRANT. In city planning, one of four parts of an area.

RAMPARTS. Raised fortifications around a place to aid in its defense.

SATELLITE CITY. In the vicinity of, and depending somewhat on, a larger city.

SECTOR. Any of the districts into which an area is divided.

SLUM. A heavily populated area in which housing and living conditions are very poor.

SUPERBLOCK. A large city block with cluster housing and a spine of shared land. As used in the Radburn plan, it included a number of culs-de-sac.

SYNDICATE. A group of individuals or organizations combining their efforts in a joint project.

TETRAHEDRON. A four-sided pyramid used as a unit in geodesic domes.

USONIA. Frank Lloyd Wright's word for the ideal city.

UTOPIA. An imaginary place that has an ideally perfect social and political system.

VISIONARY. An idealist or dreamer.

Sources of Illustrations

Numbers following the sources are page numbers

Aero Service Corporation, Division of Litton Industries 61

Aerofilms, Limited 2, 23

Ollie Atkins 63

The Bettmann Archive, Inc. 20

Consulate General of Brazil 54, 57

Metropolitan Structures of Canada, Ltd. 69 bottom

Metropolitan Structures of Canada, Ltd.; Richard Arless Associates 69 top

Information Office, Canadian Consulate General 34

Le Corbusier 49

Cumbernauld Development Corporation 65

Eggers and Higgins: Architects 95, 96

Herbert Emmerich 60 bottom

Consulate General of Finland 67

French Government Tourist Office 22, 41

Courtesy of R. Buckminster Fuller 92–93

William Hennelly 25, 26, 75, *Glossary drawings*

Carl E. Hiller 16

Information Service of India, New York 51, 52,

Italian Government Travel Office 36

Japan National Tourist Organization 35

Vincent G. Kling Associates, Architects 70, 76–77, 79

The Metropolitan Museum of Art, Harris Brisbane Dick Fund, 1947 iv

The Metropolitan Museum of Art, Rogers Fund, 1920 39 top

Netherlands Information Service 72–73

Courtesy of the New-York Historical Society, New York City 39 bottom

Omaha City Planning Department 85, 86

Department of Films and Publications, Government of Pakistan 53

Pan American Airways 42, 56

Philadelphia City Planning Commission 80–81

Chamber of Commerce of Greater Pittsburgh 83

Paul Rice for New York City Department of Buildings 14–15

Drawings by James S. Rossant. A Joint Venture comprising Harrison and Abramovitz; Philip Johnson and John Burgee; Conklin and Rossant 88, 89

San Francisco Convention and Visitors Bureau 24

Louis B. Schlivek for the Regional Plan Association 7, 8, 13, 33

Standard Oil of New Jersey Collection, University of Louisville Photographic Archives 4–5, 9, 10–11, 12

Clarence S. Stein 60 top

Tandy Industries, Inc. 91

Wide World Photos 6

Reproduced from *The Living City* by Frank Lloyd Wright, copyright 1958, by Horizon Press, with the permission of the publishers 47

Bibliography

GENERAL REFERENCES ON HISTORY, ARCHITECTURE, FORMS,
PROBLEMS OF CITIES, AND THEORIES OF PLANNING:

BACON, EDMUND N. *Design of Cities*. New York: Viking, 1967.
Probably the most beautiful book in the field, with drawings,
plans, and photographs in color and black and white.

CROSBY, THEO. *Architecture: City Sense*. New York: Reinhold, 1965
(paperback). A small book, easy to read and well illustrated with
good photographs and plans.

GRUEN, VICTOR. *The Heart of Our Cities*. New York: Simon and
Schuster, 1964 (paperback). Describes the best in city revitalization
and some of the European new towns.

HALPRIN, LAWRENCE. *Cities*. New York: Reinhold, 1963. Handsome
photographs of good examples of the modern cityscape.

HILBERSEIMER, L. *The Nature of Cities*. Chicago: Paul Theobald, 1955.
A comprehensive historical survey with illustrations.

HOSKEN, FRANCISCA P. *The Language of Cities*, New York: Macmillan,
1968. A good photographic presentation.

HOWARD, EBENEZER. *Garden Cities of Tomorrow*. London: Faber and
Faber, 1965 (paperback). Originally published in 1898 as *Tomorrow:
A Peaceful Path to Real Reform*, it outlines theories that were the
basis for the New Town movement in Britain and the United
States.

JACOBS, JANE. *The Death and Life of Great American Cities*. New York:
Vintage Books, 1961 (paperback). Lively and readable theories
that conflict with those of many of today's city planners.

KORN, ARTHUR. *History Builds the Town*. London: Lund, Humphries,
1953. A thorough history of towns and cities, giving causes for
their rise and location. Drawings, plans, photographs.

MOHOLY–NAGY, SIBYL. *Matrix of Man: An Illustrated History of Urban
Environment*. New York: Praeger, 1968. A historical approach to
the form and appearance of cities, with handsome format and
excellent illustrations.

MUMFORD, LEWIS. *The City in History*. New York: Harcourt, 1961 (paperback). A highly detailed history with good illustrations.

SCULLY, VINCENT. *American Architecture and Urbanism*. New York: Praeger, 1969. A handsome, well-illustrated book stressing the architectural aspect of American cities.

SPREIREGEN, PAUL D. *Urban Design: The Architecture and Design of Towns and Cities*. New York, McGraw-Hill, 1965. Another book stressing the architectural aspect of cities. Hundreds of sketches by the author make it fascinating browsing.

STEIN, CLARENCE S. *Toward New Towns for America*. Cambridge: M.I.T. Press, 1966 (paperback). The foremost proponent and planner of U.S. new towns describes and illustrates them.

TUNNARD, CHRISTOPHER. *The City of Man*. New York: Scribners, 1953. A social history stressing forms of cities.

TUNNARD, CHRISTOPHER, AND REED, HENRY HOPE. *American Skyline*. New York: New American Library, 1956 (paperback). An easy-to-read, chronological approach to city growth and forms in the United States, with photographs and sketches.

WRIGHT, FRANK LLOYD. *The Living City*. New York: New American Library, 1963 (paperback). Wright's theoretical Broadacre City described with his own drawings of details.

ZUCKER, PAUL. *Town and Square: From the Agora to the Village Green*. New York: Columbia University Press, 1959. A well-illustrated book emphasizing the use of open spaces in European and American cities.

OTHER BOOKS WRITTEN SPECIFICALLY FOR YOUNG PEOPLE:

HIRSCH, S. CARL. *Cities Are People*. New York: Viking, 1968.

HOAG, EDWIN. *American Cities: Their History and Social Development*. Philadelphia: Lippincott, 1969.

MUNZER, MARTHA E. *Planning Our Town*. New York: Knopf, 1964.

SCHWARTZ, ALVIN. *Old Cities and New Towns*. New York: Dutton, 1969.

Appendix

Bachelor's Programs in City Planning

Arkansas, University of
  College of Arts and Sciences
  Fayetteville, Arkansas 72701
  A.B. in urban studies

Ball State University
  Program in Regional and Urban Planning
  Muncie, Indiana 47306
  B.S. in regional and urban planning

Boston University
  Metropolitan College
  755 Commonwealth Avenue
  Boston, Massachusetts 02215
  Bachelor of Applied Science in urban
  affairs

Briarcliff College
  Urban Studies
  Briarcliff College
  Briarcliff Manor, New York, 10510
  A.B. in urban studies

California, University of
  College of Environmental Design
  Berkeley, California 94720
  A.B. in environmental design

California State Polytechnic College
  Department of Environmental Design
  Pomona, California 91766
  B.S. in urban planning

California State Polytechnic College
  School of Architecture
  San Luis Obispo, California 93401
  B.S. in city and regional planning

Case Western Reserve University
  Environmental Studies
  Cleveland, Ohio 44106
  A.B. in urban and environmental studies

Cincinnati, University of
  College of Design, Architecture and Art
  2930 Woodside Place
  Cincinnati, Ohio 45221
  Bachelor of Community Planning

Dartmouth College
  City Planning/Urban Studies Program
  Hanover, New Hampshire 03755
  A.B. major in urban studies

Georgia State University
  Department of Real Estate and Urban
    Affairs
  33 Gilmer Street, S.E.
  Atlanta, Georgia 30303
  B.B.A. in real estate and urban affairs
  B.S. in urban life, specialization in land
    development

Illinois, University of
  College of Engineering
  P.O. Box 4348
  Chicago, Illinois 60680
  B.S. in urban systems engineering or in
    transportation systems engineering

Illinois, University of
  College of Fine and Applied Arts
  208 Mumford Hall
  Urbana, Illinois 61801
  Bachelor of Urban Planning

Illinois Institute of Technology
  Department of Architecture
  School of Architecture and Planning
  Chicago, Illinois 60616
  B. Arch. with planning option

Indiana University of Pennsylvania
  Department of Geography
  Indiana, Pennsylvania 15701
  A.B. in geography

Iowa State University
Department of Landscape Architecture
Ames, Iowa 50010
B.S. in urban planning

Kent State University
Department of Geography and Geology
Kent, Ohio 44240
B.S. in pre-planning

Louisville, University of
Urban Studies Center
Louisville, Kentucky 40208
Special certificate in community development

Mankato State College
Urban Studies Center
Mankato, Minnesota 56001
B.S. in urban studies

Massachusetts Institute of Technology
School of Architecture and Planning
77 Massachusetts Avenue
Cambridge, Massachusetts 02139
B.S. in art and design, city planning option

Michigan State University
School of Urban Planning and Landscape Architecture
East Lansing, Michigan 48823
B.S. in urban planning

North Carolina, University of
Department of Geography
Greensboro, North Carolina 27412
A.B. in geography with option or concentration in urban regional planning studies

Oregon, University of
School of Architecture and Allied Arts
Eugene, Oregon 97403
Urban development option in School of Community Service and Public Affairs

Rutgers University
Department of Urban Planning and Policy Development
305 Murray Hall, Queen's Campus
New Brunswick, New Jersey 08903

A.B. with an option in city and regional planning
A.B. with a major in urban studies and community development

St. Anselm's College
Geography Department
Manchester, New Hampshire 03102
A.B. in urban studies or in geography (concentration in planning)

St. Peter's College
Urban Studies Program
2641 Kennedy Boulevard
Jersey City, New Jersey 07306
B.S. in urban studies

Shaw University
School of Urban Sciences
Raleigh, North Carolina 27602
B.S. in urban sciences (emphasis in planning)

Southeastern Louisiana College
Department of Geography
Hammond, Louisiana
A.B. in urban studies

Southern Illinois University
Earth Science Department
Edwardsville, Illinois 62025
A.B. in geography (concentration in planning or in public administration and planning)

Southwestern Louisiana, University of
Department of Social Studies
Lafayette, Louisiana 70501
A.B. in geography, city and regional planning option

Tuskegee Institute
Department of Architecture
Tuskegee Institute, Alabama 36088
B.Arch., emphasis on urban planning

Utah State University
College of Humanities and Arts
Logan, Utah 84321
B.S. in environmental planning

Virginia, University of
School of Architecture
Charlottesville, Virginia 22904
Bachelor of city planning (five years)

Washington, University of
College of Architecture and Urban
Planning
Seattle, Washington 98105
A.B. in urban planning

Washington University
College of Arts and Sciences
St. Louis, Missouri 63130
A.B. in urban studies

Canadian Schools

Manitoba, University of
Faculty of Architecture
Winnipeg 19, Manitoba
Diploma in city planning (one year)

Toronto, University of
School of Architecture
Toronto 5, Ontario
Diploma in urban and regional planning
(one year)

Two-Year Preprofessional Programs

Community College of Baltimore
Urban Affairs Department
2901 Liberty Heights Avenue
Baltimore, Maryland 21215
A.A. — urban development assistant

Cuyahoga Community College
Urban Planning Technology
Metropolitan Campus
Cleveland, Ohio 44115
One-year certificate in urban technology
with concentration in planning and
development
Associate diploma in urban technology
with concentration in planning and
development

Essex Community College
Social Science Division
Baltimore, Maryland 21221
A.A. — urban development assistant

Harford Junior College
Graphic Arts Technology Program
401 Thomas Run Road
Bel Air, Maryland 21014
A.A. in graphic arts technology

Borough of Manhattan Community College
Government Administration Program
The City University of New York
New York, New York 10010
A.A.S in government administration

Merritt College
Community Planning Program
5714 Grove Street
Oakland, California 94609
A.A. in community planning

Mohawk College of Applied Arts and
Technology
Community Planning Department
220 Dundurn Street, South
Hamilton, Ontario, Canada
A.A.S. — community planning technician

State University College, Delhi, New York
Urban and Regional Planning
State University College
Delhi, New York 13753
A.A.S. in planning and urban affairs

North Shore Community College
Public Environmental Health Technology
Program
Beverly, Massachusetts 01915
A.A. in public environmental health
technology

Community College of Philadelphia
Department of Human Services Careers
34 South Eleventh Street
Philadelphia, Pennsylvania 19107
A.A.S. in urban affairs technology

San Bernardino Valley College
  Department of Geography
  701 South Mount Vernon Avenue
  San Bernardino, California 92403
  Certificate in planning or in urban
    redevelopment and public housing
  A. A. in planning or in urban
    redevelopment and public housing

Sheridan College of Applied Arts and
    Technology
  Community Planning Department
  98 Church Street, East
  Brampton, Ontario, Canada
  A.A.S — community planning technician

Toledo, the University of
  Social Work Technology Program
  2801 West Bancroft Street
  Toledo, Ohio 43606
  A.A. in social work technology

Washtenaw Community College
  Urban Technology Program
  P.O. Box 345
  Ann Arbor, Michigan 48107
  A.A. in urban technology

Washington Technical Institute
  Urban Development Assistant Program
  4100 Connecticut Avenue, N.W.
  Washington, D.C. 20008
  A.A. — urban development assistant

Index

Acropolis, 19
Aesthetic quality, 28, 32-33, 40, 66
Agora, 19
Alaska, 58, 90
Amsterdam (Netherlands), 32
Anchorage, Alas., 58, 90-91
Ann Arbor, Mich., 22
Apartment houses, 29-30, 33, 46, 48, 52, 57, 59, 62, 66, 68, 78-80, 82, 87, 94-96
Aust, Alden, 74, 84

Babylon; Babylonia, 19, 20, 25, 37
Bacon, Edmund N., 74, 78
Baltimore, Md., 21
Bath, England, 2
Battery Park City, N.Y.C., 87-89
Boise, Ida., 22
Boston, Mass., 21, 32, 74
Brasilia (Brazil), 52, 54-57
Bridges, 24, 40
Broadacre City, 46-48

California, 58
Canada, 58, 68-69
Castle towns, 21, 23
Cathedral towns, 21-23
Champaign, Ill., 22
Chandigarh (India), 50-52
Charlotte, N.C., 22
Chartres (France), 22-23
Chicago, Ill., 30, 31, 74, 84
Cincinnati, O., 74
Circulation. See Traffic and traffic solutions
Cities: history and growth, 3, 17-22; crisis, 27-29; new, 3, 29, 50-69; see also names of cities and plans; specific concepts

City and community centers, 45, 55, 62-63, 66-69, 78-80, 82-86, 94
Cleveland, O., 74
Climate control, 87-91
Cluster plan, 62
Cologne (Germany), 20
Columbia, Md., 58, 62-63, 68
Contemporary City, 48-50
Costa, Lucio, 55
Coventry (England), 71
Cumbernauld (Scotland), 64-65
Curvilinear plan, 26, 61

Domed city, 92-93
Dover Castle (England), 23
Doxiadis, Constantinos, 52
Dresden (Germany), 71
Duluth, Minn., 22

Education, 22, 30, 31, 58, 62-63
Eggers and Higgins, 94
Egypt, 18-19
Ellicott, Andrew, 39
Emmerich, Herbert, 60
Ervi, Aarne, 66
Europe, 19-21, 26, 32

Feudalism, 21
Financial influences, 32, 40
Financing, 74, 80, 87
Finland, 58, 66-67
Florence (Italy), 20
Forum, 19
Foster City, Calif., 58
Frankfort-am-Main (Germany), 58
Fuller, R. Buckminster, 92

Garden Cities, 43-45, 59, 61; *see also* New town movement

Germany, 58

Government cities, 18-19, 22, 50-56

Government subsidization, 61, 74, 80, 87

Great Britain, 58, 64-65

Greece, 19, 37

Greenbelt towns, 58, 61

Greenbelt, Md., 61

Greendale, Wis., 61

Greenhills, O., 61

Gridiron plan, 25, 37, 39, 75

Guatemala, 21

Hartford, Conn., 74

Haussmann, Georges Eugene, 40

High-rise buildings, 29-30, 33, 46, 48, 52, 57, 62, 66, 68, 78-80, 82, 94-96

Hilversum (Netherlands), 58

Hippodamus, 37

Housing, 7, 29-30, 33, 46, 48, 51-52, 55, 57, 59, 62-63, 66-69, 74, 78-80, 82, 87-88, 94-96

Howard, Ebenezer, 43-45, 58-59, 63

India, 50-51

Industry, 13, 18, 27-28, 30, 43, 62, 66, 68, 82, 84, 90

Integration, 87

Islamabad (Pakistan), 52-53

Jefferson, Thomas, 38

Kitimat (Canada), 58

Land use, 29

Landmarks, 32-33

Le Corbusier (Jeanneret, Charles Edouard), 48-52, 94

Lee, Richard C., 74

L'Enfant, Pierre Charles, 38-39

Leningrad (USSR), 32

Letchworth (England), 44

Lincoln, Neb., 22

Linear (spinal) plan, 25-26

Logue, Edward, 74

London (England), 20, 26, 32, 64, 71

Maryland, 58, 61

Megalopolis, 26

Mexico, 21

Mies van der Rohe, Ludwig, 68

Miletus (Greece), 37

Military influences, 19, 23

Montreal (Canada), 30, 34, 58

Morocco, 16, 18

Moscow (USSR), 26, 48

Mumford, Lewis, 44, 59

Naples (Italy), 20

Nehru, Jawaharlal, 50

Netherlands (Holland), 32, 58, 71-73

New cities. *See* Cities

New Haven, Conn., 32, 74

New Jersey, 58, 59

New town movement, 58-69; *see also* Cities: new; Garden Cities

New York City, 6, 31, 33, 59, 87-89, 92-93

New York State, 59

Niemeyer, Oscar, 55

North Africa, 48

Nuns' Island (Canada), 30, 58, 68-69

Ohio, 58

Omaha, Neb., 32, 74, 84-86

Pakistan, 50-53

Paris (France), 20, 31, 40-42, 49

Parks, 29, 31, 38, 43, 48, 55, 59, 75, 87, 95

Pei, I. M., 80

Penn, William, 75

Philadelphia, Pa., 32, 70, 74-81

Pittsburgh, Pa., 32, 74, 82-83

Planners. *See* individual name entries

Plans, types of. *See* Curvilinear, Gridiron, Radioconcentric, Spinal plans; specific plans

Pollution, 5, 27-28, 55, 82, 92

Population density, 3, 27, 29, 90, 95

Providence, R.I., 74

Radburn, N.J., 51, 58-61

Radial plan. *See* Radioconcentric plan